A Life of Growth Through the Heart of the Horse

Cryshtal Avera

Copyright 2013 Cryshtal Avera

TABLE OF CONTENTS

Life is THE classroom

PERSONAL LESSONS IN SELF JUDGEMENT

LIFE IS PERFECT...(though not usually easy)

RIDING FOR TOMORROW...OVERCOMING CHAUVINISTIC MOMENTS

LETTING GO OF MY AGENDA

COMING FULL CIRCLE

BEGINNING MY JOURNEY AS A PARELLI INSTRUCTOR; Real Self Growth

THINK ABOUT WHAT YOU THINK ABOUT, NO REALLY

ASKING FOR HELP

BEING THE HORSEMAN I ALWAYS WANTED TO BE

THE BEAUTY IN BEING HUMAN

WOMEN AND MARES

PEELING BACK THE LAYERS OF SELF GROWTH

LEARNING TO SURRENDER

PRESSURE IS A GIFT

WAITING = CONNECTING = EXTROVERT CHALLENGE

SOARING WITH EAGLES

MAKING A SHIFT

ENDING = ONLY THE BEGINNING

PIVOT POINTS

LIFE IS THE MASTER CLASS

SMILING COUNTS

HUNKER DOWN

PURPOSE BORNE LEADERSHIP

LIFE IS PERFECT REVISITED & SELF LOVE

YOU GOTTA KNOW WHEN TO HOLD 'EM...

HURRY UP AND WAIT - 100 cattle became my teachers

SIMPLY ALLOW...

ABOUT THE AUTHOR

Life is THE classroom

Do you believe we each have a purpose for being alive? Do you wonder what yours is? Do you look for signs and ask, "what am I supposed to do"? During challenges or hard times, do you wonder how to determine what the best decision is?

Me too...I began asking all those questions in my early 20s and the last 15 years have been an amazing journey of experience, growth, setbacks, challenges, and living.

I believe we all have a specific purpose based on our strengths, passions, and values. We all have a unique path.

Mine has shown up with writing at the core and through horsemanship, specifically with an organization focused on relationships that has a heartfelt mission to "make the world a better place for horses and humans". Also, my non horse related small business has offered so many gifts that showed up as huge struggles.

My wish for this book is to share stories and awarenesses that resonate or trigger some awareness for you to recognize who you are, authentically, and what your path; your purpose is.

What are your strengths, passions, and values? What are you drawn to consistently? What do you find yourself dreaming about or doing regardless of whether you're getting paid? What feeds your soul?

I'd like to take you along on my journey of "aha moments" and realizations that I've been writing about for the last few years.

My calling is to continue to look for the lessons in every moment and help others see them too, as well as recognizing within your soul that you already know who you are...just listen

Every experience in life is an opportunity to learn and grow. Look it in the face and say THANK YOU, I'm so glad you've come.

This first story is about my decision to pursue the professional track through the Parelli Natural Horsemanship Program. I had a lot of self doubt about whether I had the skills and abilities to do this, but something in my heart told me to go for it when the opportunity came up. I was at a place of beginning to recognize doors in life open (and close) for a reason and had decided I'd be open to those. I gave myself permission to feel whatever feelings came up, be gentle on myself and see where this took me.

PERSONAL LESSON IN SELF JUDGEMENT

I recently completed the 1 Star Instructor Course at the Parelli Center in Florida and had yet another life changing experience and opportunity for personal growth. There were many wonderful lessons, but the one I really absorbed was about self judgement and judgement of others. I, of course, thought I was past this and "got it". However, I discovered many situations where I wanted others to hurry up and do what I thought needed to happen, simulations where I wanted the person talking to do what I thought they were supposed to be doing. Oooohhh, not a good feeling to see this in myself. I had gone Right Brained Introvert, as I have discovered I often do when I go to the Center (in new environments and learning situations) and, being that I was in such a safe, supportive environment, allowed myself to sit with it. So I was able to really observe what was going on for me internally. I also realized just how judgmental I am of myself and truly how judging myself and others go hand in hand. I guess I've kinda overlooked judging myself over the years and decided it was okay, but have always been very diligent about not wanting to judge others. Well, guess what. I now see that where there's one, so there's the other. If I'm willing to judge myself, I'm also judging others. Though that may be on a subconscious level, it's absolutely happening. What a realization. I'm still marinating on this, but definitely understand how the two things go hand in hand and am committed to letting go of all the self judgement I carry around. The Parelli Center is such an amazing place to be supported in being exactly where we're at in our journey and I see over and

9

over how Parelli really is WAY MORE THAN RIDING.

*learn more about humanalities through www.parellinaturalhorsetraining.com

This next light bulb moment came when I was sitting in the paddock with my horse feeling like the world was caving in and I couldn't find the energy to look for a way to fix it. I have a small business and had been sued, couldn't pay all the bills, and it looked like we were going to lose it. I was worried about all the debt, our house, my husband...and feeling really guilty for all of it. I had jumped in at the age of 24 without enough thought and planning and it was finally catching up with me. Through my horsemanship studies with Parelli I had been hearing Linda Parelli talk about life being perfect. As I sat there, with no hope and so much fear (after calling my mom and crying for a bit), I recognized what "life is perfect" is all about. I had a choice to make. I could continue to be hopeless or I could recognize this needed to happen in my life. There was a lesson in it somewhere. Because of this recognition, I was able to decide that every day was a gift and I could choose to enjoy it and let go of the worries. The end result was necessary in my life and I was able to snap out of it and be present in my life again. The challenge I was facing had nothing to do with my horse, but through my horse and the Parelli program I was able to find an opportunity to learn and grow.

LIFE IS PERFECT...(though not usually easy)

Do you recognize times in your life where big growth is coming? Like it or not, it's coming. Well, I'm there again and this time I recognize it. In the past I've had real difficulty with these periods, because I couldn't see what was happening...couldn't find the gift and the opportunity. Over the years I've taken baby steps and learned little by little to look for the gift and the opportunity. This time I'm fully aware it is here. It is no less challenging for me emotionally, but I am committed to staying with it and asking for the growth so I can head in that direction. One interesting aspect of this "brick upside the head" experience is that my horse has major pain, it turns out from an old injury. For the last couple weeks I've been struggling with a kidney issue and my pain is almost exactly mirrored in her body...her pain. Whoa! Talk about marinating on it; I'm fully steeping in this one to get the lesson. I'm being forced to slow down and let my body heal. I don't slow down easily. Why am I kicking and screaming on this one? It's clear my body needs rest; turns out my mind needs to slow down for my body to. Parelli teaches that Extroverts need to move their feet to think...hmmm. Without being able to move physically, I'm driving myself crazy mentally. I have taken a close look at my current mantras..."self worth" and "surrender" and realized I'm not honoring either. Today, I'm committing to both again. I'll be taking my mare, Jesse, to soak in the ocean and looking for some healing for both of us. I've realized she is physically unable to advance in some areas I've been pushing her in; all for my personal advancement in the Parelli Levels. But, life is perfect and I have another partner that is strong as an ox and super willing. Okay Universe, I'm listening. Bring it on.

This next story is from a session with my horse, Jesse, in 2011. You'll see as you read how I have struggled with self judgement and learning to be gentle with me. The reflections from my horse as I've learned to be gentle with her and put her needs first showing me the TRUTH about how I'm treating myself have been such great growth opportunities. Do you allow the people, animals, and experiences in life to offer you authentic reflections of yourself?

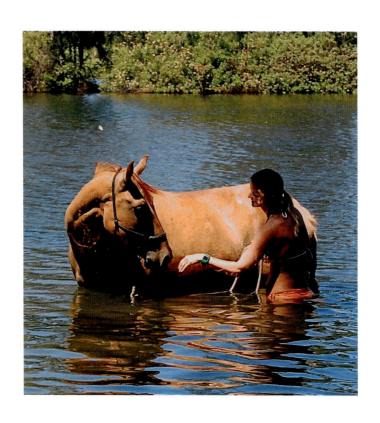

RIDING FOR TOMORROW; OVERCOMING CHAUVINISTIC MOMENTS

I had a recent ride where I really had to talk myself out of my chauvinism moment by moment. I was all set to ride the clover leaf pattern in the arena for session 3 of seven. Well, the arena was closed due to recent heavy rains and I could only walk a bit, so I started with that. There were thresholds to some surrounding equipment and activity and we had a nice slow start while Jesse gained her confidence. I decided to head to the front field for some cantering from point to point and circles around the trees. Jesse does well with open spaces as a Left Brained Introvert and I didn't think twice about her being worried. There were people around, so my ego got a bit involved and thought it was a great time for people to be able to see what we've accomplished through Parelli. Well...immediately Jesse started pulling toward home; I mean really pulling. I started going with her but doing more...so we'd do circles and almost spins always ending up back in the direction we'd started. I did this all over the field keeping to a walk and trot and she was getting more agitated. I checked my emotional state and I was still balanced, so I kept going. I had been moving with her closer to home, still using the me too strategy and eventually headed back out towards the back of the open field to see where she was regarding circling the tree. Every time she'd pull toward home, I'd support her and keep going in circles. This seemed to be working and I decided it was time to go back to trotting the circle at least once with less than 3 corrections which was my original plan when we headed out to that tree. Well, she started shutting down so I went back to point to point with the plan to get her motivated again, then go back to the circle. Next, as we were going from one tree to another, she spooked BIG. Actually took off; not something I'm used to experiencing with this calm, slow, relaxed horse. I looked back and didn't see anything that could have spooked her so I decided to ignore it and go on with the plan. Can you see all the places I missed clues? From this point, she got pretty tense and her head went up; eyes got wide.

I recognized that we were in Right Brained Introvert territory; real close to explosion. I realized I better change my strategy. But, I really wanted to accomplish my initial goal and started negative self talk about what would Pat do; what would Linda do and that at this point I should be able to get it done...etc, etc, etc. But, I could picture lessons/thoughts of wisdom from Linda and Pat like, " if the relationship is broken, do not go forward until it is fixed"..."is your horse confident and relaxed?" "I'm riding for tomorrow". Okay; I knew I had to put her first and deal with me later. I changed my plan to RETREAT figuring I'd find the place where she got confident again. Took us going almost all the way home before she relaxed a bit and stopped spooking. I had a lot to think about but reminded myself to do my thinking at night and feeling during the day.

I untacked my horse, apologized to her, turned her out and went to sit in the paddock with her. I wanted to see if there were any clues as to what had happened. Here's what happened next. She found a spot and pee'd. Now, I'm not sure if this was her main issue but twice in the distant past she started acting right brained and something told me to take the saddle off. She immediately pee'd and went back to relaxed. Did I miss that here? Gonna think about it for later. I realized that no matter what the cause was, I had not been the leader she needed. I had missed something and had struggled with putting my goals ahead of her needs. I decided to be gentle with me since I was able to have a conversation with myself and ultimately backed off. So, I'm pleased but not satisfied. I need to get it quicker next time and I have accepted that my ego is still powerful. When I showed up for the evening feeding, my horse called to me as I arrived. She rarely does this, so it was super meaningful.

LETTING GO OF MY AGENDA

So, here I am at another big breakthrough after having had the honor of asking Linda and Pat Parelli a question at our Instructor Online Event and getting wonderful guidance. After I typed the email question and read and re read it to be sure I didn't sound stupid or wasn't asking something I should already know, I closed my eyes and pressed send. I'd been struggling with the puzzle for a while and was trying different things without any clear progress and saw the opportunity to get guidance from the masters. So I put aside my insecurities and asked the question. "Should I NOT get on a home raised older gelding who is showing major dominance during saddling? How do I balance being progressive enough with taking the time it takes?" They had time for one last question and it was mine! The answer was a resounding NO, do not get on while he is showing dominance. This gave me permission (from myself) to be able to be clear and not take input from people around who might think (or should I say who I decided must think) I should just get on and make him see who's boss. I knew he needed progress, but just couldn't be clear on how I should go about setting that up to happen in the most savvy way. Linda went on to tell me to really read about her horse Allure and discussed Left Brained Extroverts. Well, I'd had Taxi's horsenality report done and it showed Left Brained Introvert. I must've been preoccupied the day I answered the horsenality questionnaire and had not felt quite right about it. But, I'm not comfortable

20

asking for do overs and had held back form requesting that. After Linda's clear guidance I picked up the phone right away and called. Of course I was graciously offered the do over and his report came back clear...Left Brained Extrovert. Linda said the horsenality reports are really the missing link and to follow it to a "t". The thing that was really HUGE for me that Linda said was to really let go of my agenda and be sure to put the horse's needs first. Now, this was something I'd been saying and would've spouted off to people I'm sure...and truly believed in. But, I hadn't really absorbed it yet. I have a lot of AGENDA with all my goals to enter the mastery program, achieve L4 and beyond... study with Linda, study with Pat, learn to work cows with Pat, etc, etc. I wouldn't have labeled my GOALS as AGENDA before, but when I get the opportunity for specific guidance from Linda Parelli, I'm taking notes, listening to every word and doing as she says. This is an opportunity for me to have real growth and bypass a lot of ups and downs / trials and errors...so, I'm taking advantage of it and getting every lesson I can from it. I sat with that phrase (briefly...though there was a lot of thinking quickly happening for this Right Brained Extrovert/Left Brained Extrovert). I saw that my goals had become my agenda and the truth was that I had somewhere along the way decided that if my goals were with Parelli, they didn't qualify as AGENDA being put before the horse's needs. I was still doing what I thought Parelli would expect from me to be a part of the team/family and had been putting purpose before principles. Ouch. Difficult to say even now; I don't wanna be that person. Having that realization, I gave myself a good talking to, got real clear that my entry into the externship and Level 4 achievements can not be the number one focus and set to putting together a new plan and way of thinking that included going to Allure's page, getting the new horsenality report and a plan to go back and soak in everything Linda has put out about Allure. Something happened to me that really changed. It's one of those things you don't know until you really know and there you are, finally. For the first time, I found myself hoping something goes wrong so I can implement strategies and laughing about it. I got this concept before, but didn't know that I hadn't really absorbed and embodied it. The first session with Taxi after Linda's advice proved incredible culminating in me getting on bareback! This horse had just been pinning his ears and even kicking out if I was doing anything in zone 3, literally 2 days before. On this day, he put him self in place next to the tailgate and invited me to get on. This is a horse who has bucked me off once and who others have approached me about saying he's unpredictable and to be careful. I now see it is all Left Brained Extrovert behavior and is very predictable. I also had similar experiences with my Left Brained Introvert mare, Jesse, who brought me to this journey and is my treasure that continues to teach me so much. It really is amazing how simple (but not easy) this is when we, the humans, get it and grow from our experiences. Also, I have a new appreciation for how quickly change can happen when we get it right. It doesn't have to be a long drawn out process, though we do have to be prepared to wait if it takes a while. These are the moments where I'm so excited and proud to be a part of the Parelli family and want to shout from the mountain tops all about how Parelli is changing my life and making me a better person. And, oh yeah, helping me get better with horses. WAY MORE THAN RIDING! WAY MORE THAN what we do at the ranch or barn...ALL ABOUT CONSTANT LEARNING AND GROWTH. All about the journey. Savvy on...

COMING FULL CIRCLE

Have you ever had a Deja Vous moment that just came out of nowhere? I was recently having a rather exciting ride on my mare and one popped up. She is in what I call "high heat" and seemed to be feeling very Left Brained Extrovert and having Right Brained Extrovert moments; some extreme moments in both quadrants. I had started my time with her at liberty and her Left Brained Introvert self was still there until we left home. It was feeding time and she's in season. Once we headed away from home for our session, she got really BIG. Not too terribly long ago, I might have decided to get off and play with her on the ground, but I felt like I could ride what she was offering and wanted to give it a go. I've been really studying Left Brained Extrovert strategies and all that I can find on Linda's Parelli Connect page with Allure and Westpoint, and have the horsenality report on Taxi, a Left Brained Extrovert. So I matched her energy and off we went. She was most interested in winking at all the boys we passed and boy did it get interesting when we passed the herds and all those geldings! I pulled on my Left Brained Extrovert side and tried to think quick and match her. I was having quite a lot of fun and just using this ride as an opportunity to test myself and see if I had the strategies and abilities to give Jesse what she needed in a leader. An hour or so into the ride, as we were finding our way around the ranch, I realized we were in a spot where I had my last upsetting, scary, frustrating ride on Jesse a few years back that was my breaking

24

point. She was bucking and mad and her focus was clearly on getting away from me. Interestingly enough, she had been in heat and it was feeding time that day. That was the point where I couldn't take any more and didn't know who to turn to or what to do. It really affected me emotionally because I so wanted my horse to just love me. I had thought of finding a better leader for her, but couldn't imagine the possibility of handing her over and not knowing what would happen to her. I had been really down on myself. I had finally realized I had to fix me and recognized I was gonna have to go great lengths (and distances) to do so. I realized I always went to the Parelli Program when I had problems and thought, "I wonder what I could accomplish if I commit to this program". My horse's needs and my desperation were finally more important than what people around me thought (what I thought they thought) or said about Parelli and my journey began. I pulled that Level 2 pack off the shelf and never looked back. Having listened to Pat Parelli's audio cd on progressiveness, I've been reflecting on all this and looking at my goals, asking myself if I'm progressive and if I have a balance where I can put the horse's needs first. I believe I teeter back and forth between progressive and non progressive and realize this life lesson and life skill is like all the others I seek as I move through my journey. It will likely come and go. I will likely find growth in this area at times and will also likely lose a little ground at times. Isn't it amazing how when we get some of these lessons and understandings they start to really affect all our struggles? Just having the true acceptance and understanding that I won't ever "get there" and that I really need to focus on the journey and EXPECT A

LOT, ACCEPT A LITTLE, REWARD OFTEN...for me, has been transformational in every aspect of my life. I keep saying Parelli is life changing & it continues to be true. I currently feel like I'm on a roller coaster with so many wonderful lessons and opportunities for growth coming my way and it's exhilarating! It's so cool how this is mirrored in my horsemanship journey, as well and am loving the confidence I've begun to achieve. It feels like there's a domino effect in place; each great lesson brings another new opportunity. I am truly discovering what it feels like to live life with Passion and follow my dreams; to honor my true self. I am starting to attain those mantras I currently have on my vision board: SURRENDER & SELF WORTH. THANK YOU PAT AND LINDA AND THE INCREDIBLE PARELLI FAMILY! What a ride!

BEGINNING MY JOURNEY AS A PARELLI INSTRUCTOR; REAL SELF GROWTH

My first few months as a Parelli 1 Star Junior Trainee Instructor have been amazing, super busy, and life transforming in ways I couldn't have even imagined! I am seeing daily, the changes in me, and am so very grateful! For me, the thought of becoming an Instructor started somewhere during the Parelli Fast Track course in April, 2010. I had signed up with a strong focus on it being about my horsemanship and truly didn't think I had the ability or skills, and doubted I ever could, to become a Parelli Instructor. Pat Parelli spoke to us then, giving great insight and thoughts on what we'd get from the experience. The thing I really took from that talk was "empowerment". When Pat said we'd be empowered, a light bulb went off and I thought to myself, "that's what I need". That experience proved to give me great personal insight that I needed, and boy was it challenging. I went home and the opportunity to go to the 1 Star Instructor Course came about. I had to work hard to put aside my self doubts and go for it. The 1 Star Instructor Course brought great breakthroughs and realizations on self judgement and judging others going hand in hand. Another hard look at myself and fantastic opportunity to begin really developing my self worth; something I'd discovered I was sorely lacking at this point. I've been home for a few months, offering my required free lessons and committing to remain open to the experience and all it has to offer. As I come to the end of my 50 free teaching hours and am making plans to move forward, I am truly in awe of all this experience has offered thus far. First, in helping others, there is great satisfaction. I am rediscovering how incredible that is! However, I had forgotten how much learning to teach others teaches us. I am marinating fully in that fabulous opportunity with each lesson I give. Going back to study Parelli Level 1 in preparation for teaching it well is offering me so much! The really powerful change in me is my confidence. One of my challenges being lacking self worth (very difficult to admit, still) I am so humbled and grateful that this journey with Parelli is helping me find it. My horsemanship studies intertwine with my teaching to offer such incredible progress and I am discovering how very much confidence means to my horsemanship journey. I am currently on what feels like a roller coaster ride. For the first time in my life this roller coaster ride feels RIGHT rather than like pushing a boulder uphill. My first big lesson at the Parelli Center was that I am the only one in my way when it comes to achieving my dreams and I am learning how to get out of my own way through this incredible experience thanks to Parelli! "Way more than riding" really doesn't do justice to this incredible organization and the amazing people that make up the Parelli tribe. My belief is that connecting with Parelli in some way would be great for ALL humans, regardless of whether there are horses in their lives. I suppose it already is, due to the fact that all of us Parelli students are changing for the better and walking through life in a more balanced way...CHANGING THE WORLD FOR HUMANS AND HORSES, truly.

THINK ABOUT WHAT YOU THINK ABOUT, NO REALLY

Life is just full of surprises and lots of opportunities to push our limits and expand, right? It seems I am consistently finding opportunities (or they are finding me) to focus and grow in areas of the 8 Principles or other fabulous pieces of Parelli theory. I've heard Pat Parelli say "think about what you think about" quite a few times and am really getting clear on how powerful that is. You see, I own a small business and have been gliding along loving all the time I have to focus on my Parelli studies and newly begun career path, as my business systems had begun to work smoothly without me needing to be there. I employee a great team of incredible individuals who just take care of things. I was recently on the Big Island teaching and got a letter via my handy dandy iPhone, from my property manager. My lease is up and we had been negotiating terms. I thought we'd find common ground, but no cigar. So this was the letter that ended in the words, "vacate the premises by July 31, 2011". OMG! I was with a friend I hadn't seen in a while when I got the email and tried to hold it together. I didn't sleep well and found myself focusing on the issue as I flew back home. I got the flu as soon as I arrived home and was down for about 5 days. Still worrying. After about the first week I really started stepping back from the situation and hearing those words...think about what you think about. Man, they started to resonate in a powerful way. Here I am, dealing with a major choice that will affect my source of income and I have no choice but to take action. Control has been taken away and I have to find a way to resolve the issue without losing everything. I'm having lots of "okay, let's take a deep breath" moments, I must admit, but have come to a place of strength and seeing the gifts in this. This, along with all the challenges I've faced before have prepared me by giving me skills, experience, and knowledge that I need right now. All these attributes are allowing me to think quickly in a time crunch and move toward a positive outcome. I have now begun to create options that will likely be much more successful than my current business set up and I only have that ultimatum letter to thank for kicking me into action! THINK ABOUT WHAT YOU THINK ABOUT has taken on a whole new meaning for me and once again I have relied on the Parelli program/organization and all the self awareness resources it provides to get me through a potentially scary time that has nothing to do with horses. Though I don't have a personal relationship with Linda or Pat, I hear their voices and see their words clearly and they have been key guidance for me; helping me stay on the path of progressiveness versus getting bogged down with worry or negative thoughts. I only have so many hours and so much energy and I am processing in a new way how much my thoughts can use up that time and energy and zap me if I'm not very FOCUSED on keeping my thoughts on track. MY REALITY IS WHAT I THINK ABOUT. I'm sure there's an even much deeper lesson that I'm not seeing yet, but I have been trying to use this opportunity to challenge myself to find peace in the storm as well as continue to enjoy the journey, even through the scary moments. Writing about this makes it so real and, reflecting on the person I was 5 years ago when I opened this business, I am amazed at how far I've come as a human being. This is why I am so passionate about representing Parelli to others and being a part of this program for the rest of my life. Here's an extreme situation where I could have gotten really depressed but I'm able to find the gifts and continue to enjoy my day to day life while I deal with this. Do Pat and Linda Parelli truly get how deeply they affect us? How they have given us the skills and growth to LOVE LIFE every day at times when we might otherwise find ourselves unwittingly headed down a negative path? I am feeling powerful and finding that I naturally have the tools to cope with and resolve this situation & it's due to this little self help program called Parelli. Oh yeah, and it's helping me with my horses too.

ASKING FOR HELP

Well, it's been about a month since I was given the ultimatum to vacate the unit my business currently occupies. What a whirlwind! Soon after my last story, I began participation in the Tribal Leadership Intensive Course via www.culturesync.net. I have read the book, "Tribal Leadership" at least three times since discovering it on the recommended reading list during the 1 Star Instructor Course I participated in at the Parelli Florida Campus last February. We were given a great opportunity to participate in the TLI Course through Parelli and I jumped at the chance. However, the start date came at a time when I thought I couldn't possibly take on one more thing. But, I am smitten by the Tribal Leadership concepts and knew it was an opportunity I couldn't pass up. I pushed past my doubting thoughts and dialed in for the first call. We were given some guidelines and our coaches introduced themselves. We learned more about Tribal Leadership and were given a list of outcomes we could expect from this course. Some that meant a lot to me were... Produce Outcomes and Results, People will seek you out, Manage your reputation, Connect easily with people and Declare your Core Values and Noble Cause. We were given buddy groups and heard from many of the other participants during each call. The experience of being surrounded by so many successful, positive, progressive people was powerful. For me, it was akin to how I feel when at the Parelli Campus. It's hard to put in words, but those moments of what that energy brings seems to create a shift; to clear a pathway that wasn't visible before. We were given homework, which added to the already busy lives of all of us and our coaches later talked about how this course was set up for us to really dig in to what can often feel overwhelming. This way we'd be able to really understand the concepts of being elevated to the next stage where we begin to create triads and support systems all around us. This concept excited me to no end, as I have a lot of ideas and things I want to do and don't ever envision having a life full of lazy days and only one focus. I can overwhelm myself. But, I've got a lot of living to do and loved that I'd be given tools to make it happen! So, as Linda Parelli says, life is perfect and this course came up for me exactly when I needed it. I've been given tools on how to let go of things, how to truly prioritize and still get things done and I'm peeling back the layers and seeing how to know what I absolutely have to do myself and what I can ask for help with. Let me say that again; what I can ASK FOR HELP WITH. This is the biggest piece that was missing for me. Somehow it completely escaped me that it's not only okay, but it's a good thing to ask those who love and support you for help. It makes life so much more enriched and meaningful to do things with others, honor their values and yours, as well as really learning how we are walking through the world; our reputation. It seems so simple, but I'm discovering how powerful a shift in our thinking really is. Truly, words don't give the power of this experience meaning, but I hope sharing the words I can come up with is meaningful to you. My wish is that it triggers something beautiful in your innermost being and you can dig it out and give it focus and power as I have begun to do. For me, it's an integral piece of the puzzle of my life, and my journey has taken on new meaning; not totally different meaning, but a more clear and enriching version of itself.

Regarding the major transition in my business that felt like such a BIG DEAL a month ago, I have my moments, but really have a new way of seeing the world in key areas. So, this has become an experiment for me on how well I have understood the concepts of being a true Tribal Leader; inspiring people, creating culture, creating triads and networks. I am using the tools I've been given to put a strong focus on my career as a Parelli Professional and continuing to shoot for the moon and follow my passion! The key word for me as I go through this is FUN! Gotta have fun...just like the Parelli program teaches us about with our horses.

BEING THE HORSEMAN I ALWAYS WANTED TO BE

I just completed 5 days of horsemanship study. What an experience! The first two days of lessons were on Oahu with my horse and the final 3 were on Maui at Piiholo Ranch where I leased a finished bridle horse. Yep, a finished bridle horse! The amazing "Pecan". My request was to get a horse that could teach me. Specifically, I mentioned wanting to focus on walk/canter transitions, leads, lead changes, and circling at a canter with no corrections and a casual rein. During my flight over to Maui I read an article in the "Hana Hou", the Hawaiian Airlines Magazine, titled Legend for a Day. It was perfect timing and got me thinking about something I've heard Pat Parelli say. "It's never too late to be the person you always wanted to be". I decided I would be the horseman I've always wanted to be. I even created a mantra for the weekend..."I am the legend". Now, this was not an easy thing for me to say to myself much less for me to put in writing. I am, after all, a Right Brained Extrovert/Left Brained Extrovert with a strong identification with the phrase Linda Parelli talked about when telling us about Elements of Man..."Am I okay?". This is precisely the reason I am writing it down and sending it out into the cyber world; to challenge myself and to progress. "Pecan", the horse I leased and expected all sorts of education from taught me right away that having a horse that can teach you does NOT mean he doesn't need a leader. I didn't realize I hadn't shown up fully for him, I just went about my business saying hello to everyone and marveling at the beauty of the ranch. We started with friendly game as we got to know each other and all was going well. I was swinging the stick and string over his back and began pulling it away and snapping the ground. He began moving and before I knew it I was dizzy running in circles backing up with the clinician trying to get it through my head and down to my feet to back straight and not back circles. You know those moments when it all happens so fast you can't process right away? Well, this was one of those for me. I had made an assumption that he wouldn't get bothered about anything. It wasn't what I would call an extreme moment, but it really got me thinking. We had a break and I thought about the energy and the leadership I had brought to "Pecan". I realized that I wasn't super focused and I wasn't putting him first; I was putting my fun and my human connections first. My thoughts were not fully clear and were all over the place, but in a good way. I came to discover that doesn't matter. I thought back to that article in the Hana Hou and began telling myself, "I am the horseman I always wanted to be", "I am the legend". Made me almost giggle after I looked around to be sure no one heard my thoughts and I required myself to keep focusing on that mantra. Something began to happen for me, I logically knew, and was okay with, this not being true, and was able to hear the clinicians inputs and corrections. But, at the same time, I could feel the power in that mind set. Like the surfer wrote about in his story, I didn't need to have anyone else see me that way, but did it for me, and for the horse. I had realized that when Pat Parelli says he expects us to be loyal to the horse, part of what that means is showing up as the leader the horse needs; putting the relationship first. Well, having this mantra helped me work towards fulfilling that duty. Here was a finished bridle horse with lots of life experience and I was creating issues for him until I changed my energy, my leadership. Of course, some of the challenges I began to create are challenges I see in my own horse. What feedback. And I am reminded that it's up to me what I expect and can inspire in my own horse. I can give excuses or I can flip the switch and just do it.

THE BEAUTY IN BEING HUMAN

Being Human to me means a person showing what I would, in the past, have called having issues, or something similar pointing to negativity. I now am beginning to see those moments as authentic and can see the beauty in a person allowing me to witness them; and allowing themselves to just be. By default I am also seeing the beauty in myself being authentic in those moments, versus beating myself up. I'm learning to notice and let go. I'm beginning to transcend and truly show up for myself and in my relationships in a more powerful way. Wow! What a journey these last few months have been! Moving a business and opening a second location, becoming a certified Parelli Professional, and participating in the Culture Sync courses Tribal Leadership Intensives 1 and 2. All these experiences have created a flow of opportunity for major growth that I never saw coming. Stepping into my fears with the major changes in my business and giving myself permission to have fears about living my dreams with horses and with Parelli, but go there anyway, while continuing my horsemanship journey have brought me to this place of real self acceptance. You see, I have been given tools and accountability that have led me to focus on human relationships more than I had been in a long time. I've come to see that living a meaningful life starts with real connections. Not networking. CONNECTIONS. Before I can ask a person to get involved in a project or do something with or for me, I really need to CONNECT to have anything of beauty come of it. Simultaneously, we have to find some resonance of values and a noble cause. In the Tribal Leadership Intensive Courses we have been working at listening for values in conversations with others. This has given me more of an awareness on how much I have not been truly connecting with people in my life. I had consistently been focused on me in conversations and relationships. My focus has been on things like, "what are my interests, what am I excited about, what do I want from this interaction, what do I want to say next?" Pretty self absorbed, right? For a while, I'd been thinking I had a self worth problem. I now am asking the question, "does lack of self worth sometimes mean too much self absorption?". If we are feeling less than, or seeing the world in a way that we begin to feel less than, are we being a bit self absorbed? On the flip side, if we're focused on supporting others in our lives and looking for opportunities to increase their success or happiness, it seems almost impossible to feel lack of self worth. Couple that with creating and keeping relationships based on resonant values and a noble cause, then include a project. Add to that the stability of triadic relationships and Katy bar the door! TLI 1 and 2 teachings also include creating relationships based on merit, which is helping me to see that some relationships don't make sense. This allows me to move on and not judge them, or me, but to be clear that the relationship doesn't make sense. How powerful. This time in my life and these glorious opportunities are truly helping me transition into a much more powerful place. I knew there was something missing in me and it is beginning to show up and be filled up. I now keep the following formula in my mind as I connect with other humans.

Connection & Support (WE v/s me + values & a project) + filling roles ONLY with people whose heart sings in that role = Having an ongoing CONVERSATION that generates authentic, genuine success for ALL.

I've come to this conclusion. Life is way more than a journey. It's a CONVERSATION full of inquiry. And a real gift that has come of all this human connecting is that I am truly putting the connection with my horse first and not moving forward to "do" anything if the expression isn't there. I'm getting more clear on the concept of having loyalty to our horse. The CONNECTION is everything. What does my horse need in every moment? That's the question I now ask. And I can finally focus on that without letting the worry of possible judgement from others cloud the CONVERSATION or take too much of my time. I'm not saying it's not coming up at all. I am, after all, simply human. However, I now notice it, give gratitude, and let it go.

WOMEN AND MARES

(Written in 2011)

At 34, I have begun a quest to learn about, and honor, the things about being a woman that I have lived my life resenting. My attitude has always been, "give me a pill or something to make it go away so I can get on with my life". Well, my emotions and other effects have gotten to a place over the years where I realized something had to be off; out of balance. And I am finally at a place where I am high enough on my priority list to make finding a way to feel better a priority. Also, I'm scheduled for an Externship course at the Parelli Center in Colorado next year and am committed to finding a way to get more emotionally balanced and get my hormones in check. In the past, I've gone completely Right Brained Introvert when at the Parelli Center and it gets in the way of the potential richness of the experience. I'm ready to be the human I've always wanted to be, and as a woman, must get this hormone thing worked out. The experience of being in a place where we're encouraged to be authentic and feel the feelings is amazing and each visit gets more comfortable. One aspect of my quest is beginning to really explore Chinese Medicine. I'm learning that Chinese Medicine is way more than acupuncture and am going to appointments weekly. I've also begun taking Chinese herbs and learning about lifestyle changes that can help. Food therapy is helpful. But ya know what has given me to most dramatic results? Controlling my state of mind; controlling my thoughts. Now, I give myself permission to stop for a day and rest. I use a mantra my mom taught me..."wait to worry". I notice when my energy is draining and put a strong focus on bringing it back to me, to rejuvenate me. I talk with other women about the realities of the differences in being a woman and celebrate those things. Just changing my mindset and my thoughts makes things easier. I'm also seeing my equine partner, Jesse, differently. My outlook was greatly changed through the horsenality reports and education, which helped us to get more connected. I now see her with a greater respect and appreciation. As my mother in law told me once, "remember, we're mares too". I'm not crazy just because I have different emotions on different days. Well, neither is Jesse, this beautiful Left Brained Introvert mare; my greatest teacher. She must have days where even being looked at with my focus and intention feels overbearing. I get that. She must have days where she just isn't feeling well and is more introverted than usual. She must have days where she is more emotionally sensitive than others. I have at least 7 days of being introverted and emotionally sensitive, to varying degrees, every month. Women are designed that way, so it only makes sense that mares are our mirrors in those ways to some extent, as well. There's no getting away from it. I'm ready to honor it and try harder to recognize it. Jesse challenges me to be uncomfortable and be okay. She challenges me to truly listen and communicate with her, because she'll rarely feel the same as the day before. She's a Left Brained Introvert; I'm a Right Brained Extrovert. She needs to think. I can't stop thinking...and doing. When people are watching, my ego wants to impress. She usually

44

requires me to do the exact opposite of what that would look like. If my thoughts even hint to frustration or disconnection or pushiness, she pushes back. If I use physical encouragement to get her to move, she kicks out. If I get more adamant, so does she. She doesn't give up and she won't back down if she isn't being respected and heard. I now see this description and these words and smile. I think, "now that's quite a woman". I aspire to be that kind of woman. The reward in her offering me things before I ask, or more than I ask is more fulfilling than I can find words for. Having her look at me with those ears forward, questioning, brings such joy and feels like such an accomplishment. It truly fills my heart to capacity. In those moments I'm so connected to her and so proud of me. The beauty and the amazing gift this treasured being offers me is this. I have the perfect teacher in my life. She doesn't have an ego and she doesn't hold grudges. She expects me to do what she needs and she offers the moon when I do. She is a perfect mirror, giving instant feedback. She offers endless opportunities for me to be the human, the woman, I want to be. As I begin this part of my journey with true acceptance and honor for myself, I embrace the unknown and all the moments I'll need to say "how interesting" as I continue the quest for a genuine partnership with this powerful mare. I find myself at this place again, where I am growing and changing as a human being in ways I never would have even imagined or known to imagine, had I not found Parelli. Jesse, my treasure, required me to commit to this amazing program and I have found my life passion. Way more than riding is such an understatement.

PEELING BACK THE LAYERS OF GROWTH

As I move through life and seek to become the human being I aspire to be, I find I gain clarity on things progressively. I've come to look at it as peeling back the layers. Like an onion. For example, last year I truly saw the importance of learning to control our thoughts. I understood and absorbed that our thoughts truly do create our reality. However, conceiving of it and being able to do it are sometimes two very different things. But I've come to believe that's maybe not the best way to look at it. Rather than thinking in a way that highlights how imperfect I am or the situation is, why not choose to see it as part of the process? Today, I'll get it at this level and that's how it's supposed to be. I'm exactly where I'm supposed to be. I will process this lesson in this way today, and as I grow and have more experiences, I will continue to process each lesson at a different level and with more clarity. Peeling back the layers. Regarding the concept of thoughts create our reality, I've had some key lessons. We must choose to focus on the thoughts we want to have based on the life we want. In setting my intentions for 2012 with a simple written plan, I gave myself permission to let go of the noise, meaning the worries about what I SHOULD be doing or guilt about what others might expect, or I might expect of myself. Almost on a daily basis, I consciously give myself permission to put the things that speak to my heart and make up who I am as priority. Two mantras I have for 2012 are MY THOUGHTS CREATE MY REALITY and I AM WILLING TO BE UNCOMFORTABLE TO BECOME THE HUMAN I WANT TO BE. I find many moments where those come in handy and allow me to keep moving forward. With an Externship scheduled soon, I expect to have lots of opportunities for both mantras to come in handy. The key difference in years past is that I don't have any resolutions and I don't expect to "get somewhere" by the end of the year. I have intentions based on being more clear on who I am, authentically. I have a clear vision of following my heart and an understanding and willingness to allow life to unfold as it should; without expectations of what the result will look like. I know I will be uncomfortable at times, but with the clarity of who I am beginning to truly unfold for me, I welcome those moments and have strategies on how to get through them. I am willing to be gentle with myself in the moments I don't get through the discomfort so gracefully and expect that to be part of the peeling back of the layers of my growth. I am letting go of preconceived notions of issues I think I have so I can move forward and not hold myself back with these thoughts. Through my first year as a Parelli Professional and the Culture Sync courses based on the book Tribal Leadership (an offer facilitated through Parelli) I have gained some tools that validate my beliefs in positive thinking and added strategies to actively create the life that is waiting for me. I am clear on my commitments, I am clear on my purpose (called a Leadership Declaration in the courses). I start my day with gratitude and a plan based on my values and learning needs, I end my day with gratitude and rating my ability to find balance in all areas throughout the day. Things like attitude and rejuvenating are on the list we learned to rate ourselves on and let me tell you, those were not things I had really considered and couldn't recognize, originally. I discovered there were rejuvenating moments in each day, but I didn't allow them to rejuvenate. All the noise in my head kept me from being rejuvenated. Interesting, isn't it? As I move forward into what I expect to be a life changing year, I am committed to reminding myself that each lesson is another layer and, just as in horsemanship, our life lessons will continue to unfold and we will be better for each experience. There is a gift in each one and I am finally ready to accept each one as exactly what it's supposed to be, with the knowledge that the process of my learning and growth will continue to progress. I have discovered my desire is to help others find authentic growth and hope this blog has inspired you in some way to listen to your heart and be gentle with yourself.

As Linda Parelli teaches us, learners are fragile. Just as our horses are, so are we. Finding Parelli is such a huge gift and opportunity for all of us to grow in amazing ways and be surrounded by others who share Core Values, Passion, and genuine beliefs that support is a key ingredient we all need.

LEARNING TO SURRENDER

My Mom says "let go and let God". Whatever that means to each of us, this is a powerful concept. I have always been super motivated. A person who adamantly pursues things with the attitude that there are no brick walls. In the South we have a saying. I'm like a dog with a bone; I won't let go. Through my journey with Parelli, I am learning so many wonderful life lessons. One being that there is no black and white. It brings to mind a quote by Pat Parelli, "Never say never, don't always say always, usually say usually". There are no rules, but there are principles and guidelines. My first course at the Parelli Center was the Fast Track in early 2010 and we were given a strong focus on learning to be puzzle solvers. That was such a gift and I continue to work at being a better puzzle solver. In saying all this, I'm hoping to share with you what I'm learning about surrendering. I'm learning there can be a balance between being a go getter and allowing for life to unfold exactly as it's supposed to. I'm reminded of another Parelli-ism, "become an extreme middle of the roadist". I love that! As I'm presented with day to day life, I realize we commit to the principles, values, and behaviors we want to embody and receive opportunity after opportunity to be the person we want to be. Some days we get it and some days we fall back a bit. The beauty is in the process. We must forgive ourselves and keep our commitments. I am scheduled to go the the May Externship and have been preparing for months for this to be the pinnacle of what I intend to be a life changing year. I have finally given myself permission to truly live my dreams. I have changed my thoughts from "I don't know if I'm worthy or good enough" to have a real career as a Parelli Professional" to "I am a Parelli Professional". I have claimed my journey based on my passions and what speaks to my heart. I have shifted my focus to this path with a belief that I will make a living doing the things I love. For me that is specifically helping people learn and find authentic self growth through horsemanship and my writing. So, back to the Externship. I received an email stating that I must achieve very specific horsemanship results by the end of March to ensure my spot is not filled with someone else. I have been working a plan that gets me there by mid April. What an excellent opportunity to find the balance between adamantly pursuing a goal and being able to surrender to what the Universe has in store for me. I've decided to believe I will be there, I've written my audition plans in multiple places so I can practice them constantly in my mind (we are in the middle of some very rainy/muddy weather here) and have a schedule on creating videos. I will reach out to mentors for coaching. I am letting go of any worries or doubtful thoughts that might enter my mind. I will do my best while honoring the relationship with my horse and putting that first. I will be focused and committed. I won't create a backup plan as I normally would, but I know I'll be flexible if I need to. I'm letting go of the noise in my mind and moving toward this goal as a priority. Once I get my audition results, I'll be able to look to my next step. But I am letting go of control. I believe God , the Universe, Spirit, has a bigger dream for me than I could ever dream for myself. My future is to

50

continue as a Parelli Professional and continue this journey. I give up control of how that journey unfolds. I recently read something 4 Star Parelli Professional, Kristi Smith wrote. "We only fail if we give up". So, I know I won't fail. I am blessed. I have found, at 35, the core things that make my heart sing. Now I can spend the rest of my life absorbing the experiences of moving toward those passions every day. We are told to memorize Parelli theory until it's tattooed on the back of our eyelids and I see more and more why this is recommended. Once it's ingrained in our minds, we call it forward subconsciously when we need it. As with every challenge and life experience, I am looking for the opportunities to learn and grow. Also, I am again awestruck at how the Parelli Organization, Program, and Tribe are set up to help us constantly grow and learn. I intend to enter the Mastery program in May but life is my Master Class and I'll get to Pagosa Springs soon. The format for my next learning experience may not be what I had planned on, but it will be exactly what I need. Here's to learning to surrender...

PRESSURE IS A GIFT

This journey continues to unfold in beautiful and surprising ways. The latest opportunity for growth has been through my preparation for the Externship in May. I, as a Right Brained Extrovert, have discovered pressure can really bring out fear, anxiousness, and lack of confidence. I can get quite fizzy. All those things can come together and create a self fulfilling prophecy of "I'm not good enough". I'm done with that. I'm taking charge of my thoughts and working at it daily. Now that I have gone through a 3 week period where I put constant pressure on myself to try to meet the horsemanship requirement to confirm my spot in the Externship, I'm looking back and reflecting on what challenges I can learn from and the growth opportunities. As an aside, I'd like to mention that I've been keeping a gratitude journal per the latest book by Rhonda Byrne titled, "the Magic". Also, I'm following Dr. Wayne Dyer and Tony Robbins closely right now and my focus is on gratitude and creating the life I desire with my thoughts. Becoming the human I want to be. Honorable, Inspired, Passionate, Humble. So, back to the reflections. One thing I've peeled back another layer on is The Gift of Pressure. I saw Tony Robbins talking about two performers he'd met who described the same reaction before they go on stage, but each of them called it something different. One called it anxiety and another called it happy excitement. One felt she needed therapy and help to get rid of it and another loved having it because it told him he was ready for the performance. Then, I saw Dr. Dyer talk about how we can choose to view each challenge in our lives as a gift to help us fulfill our destiny. I realized that's what I need to do. I need to change my view on pressure to label it as a gift to help me grow and look at each challenge that comes my way as a true blessing. It's up to me and I can change my life in a moment, by changing my thoughts. I have made the decision to choose to genuinely view pressure and challenges as gifts that are given to me to help me grow into the human I want to be. I am gaining more and more clarity on my core values, commitments, and who I am, so that helps. The gift in this realization before the Externship course is huge. It's gonna help me in those moments when I am pushed to the limit of my emotional and physical fitness, as well as when I'm invited to step into discomfort to grow in my horsemanship. I am going to keep a mantra close to me, "this challenge is a gift and will help me grow into the human I want to be". Each time a challenge comes my way, I will have a choice. I can move forward with worry and fear or I can move forward with gratitude and love. I am committed to choosing gratitude and love. I am so happy to go into the Externship with this realization. It will help me get the most I can from this experience. It will help me get rid of the noise that can enter this Right Brained Extrovert mind. When I feel the noise coming on, I use a technique I learned from reading "the Magic". Instead of worrying or thinking about things so much, I say THANK YOU THANK YOU THANK YOU until I can feel it in my heart and it reminds me what an amazing life full of many blessings I have. May you have the gifts of pressure and

challenges in your life to help you move forward;
further into the journey that is uniquely yours.

WAITING = CONNECTING = EXTROVERT CHALLENGE

What does waiting look like for you? Do you know? Until recently I hadn't thought too much about the details of how I wait when my introvert mare, Jesse, has that need. I made sure to take the pressure off, but didn't worry about it much past that. I'd watch for the signs that she was ready to move on and get back to it. I've come to realize that how I wait matters. Through coaching from Kristi Smith, 4 Star Parelli Instructor, using the educational resources available through Parelli, a progressive goal, and consistent reflections on self, I have discovered that as an extrovert, my waiting hasn't been what my horse, who is an introvert, needs. Interesting. What I had done was congratulate myself on understanding that she needed me to wait and given myself permission to move my feet in other ways. I'd go work on a chore, go check the water, go get the next obstacle or tool I'd need, or check my iPhone for emails, Facebook updates, etc. Something to busy myself physically while she processed. I've been experimenting with changing how I wait and it really has made a big difference in my relationship with my horse. I asked Kristi about what I'm doing and she reminded me that horsenality is not an excuse and that I have to find a way to do what my horse needs. As I began to focus on waiting = stopping completely and being there with Jesse, I created a mantra to help me..."be the Left Brained Introvert"...or Right Brained Introvert depending on the situation.

Mantras really help me focus. I've been noticing my instinct to start moving away from or all around her in those moments when Jesse needs me to wait and not put pressure on. I stop and stand and use my mantra. After a couple sessions I realized this is intertwined with connecting to Jesse's energy. I saw that it is another way to mirror my horse and match her energy. I now focus on a mantra that reminds me to be there with her; really connect and feel her energy. Did you see the movie "Avatar"? Those moments now make me feel and say to my horse, "I see you", and I really do. But there's an even greater gift. Yet again, my horse is providing the treasure of self awareness and growth. Because I am committed to meeting her needs and am focusing on waiting without pressure and on being with her, I am finding this time is wonderful for me to relax my mind. It may not quite be meditation, but it helps me chill out and take moments I haven't found the ability to do, as an extrovert, until now.

I now see honoring Jesse's introvert needs as an opportunity for moments to relax and find quiet for my very active mind. In the last two weeks my horse has rolled near me more than she has in 9 years. Each time it happens I am so honored and humbled. There is such beauty in this journey, especially in how the little things we change about ourselves can make the biggest difference for our horse.

SOARING WITH EAGLES

As the fourth week of the externship closes, I am have so many experiences and lessons learned I want to share. I have been changed for the better and know I will leave with much growth in skills, confidence, teaching skills, and self awareness. The biggest gift has become so clear to me recently. This experience is allowing me to truly soar with eagles, so to speak. I look around every day and am surrounded by amazing human beings. People who share my passion and are committed to it, but more than that, people who are truly beautiful from the inside out. Each one has a unique gift or strength and just being in their presence sets me up for success; makes me better. Surrounding ourselves with others who are what and who we want to be is a concept I have long believed in. This experience, however, is the best lesson I've gotten that shows me how true it is. Our Externship Coach, 4 Star Parelli Professional, Teri Sprague is far better than any words I have can describe. She pushes us so we stretch, but helps us not go so far we go over the cliff. She gives us guidance in the exact moment and exact situation where we can use it and, seemingly, we become better in an instant. She makes each and every one of us feel that we are capable, skilled enough, and worthy of being here and that we can do amazing things. She is changing our lives by being who she is authentically, and oh what an inspiration that is! Not to mention what an incredible horsewoman she is. It's like being at an ongoing clinic for 3 months. I am determined to remain in gratitude throughout this experience. Can you imagine being surrounded each day for 90 days, by people who are each the caliber of human being you want to be? Well, I am having that experience. Everywhere I look, I see amazing skills.

Everywhere I turn, there is support. Every day I feel lifted up by someone who is inspiring or helping me in some way. One fellow extern is helping me overcome my nerves surrounding public speaking with tips and support based on her 14 years teaching on the subject, and I am truly growing. Another gal shares some of my Right Brain tendencies and by making herself vulnerable every day so that she can grow, and by being open and honest about it, she helps me continue to put myself out there. There are key aspects to being a part of a course like this at the Parelli Campus that make a real impact.

Genuine support, mastery, passion, and dedication are a few big keys. By being at a place that exudes these things through the people who created it and those who maintain it, as well as being in a group where each person embodies each of them, creates a perfect storm of learning and BIG GROWTH! What are your dreams? What's standing in your way? Are you soaring with eagles every day? Follow your bliss...and be aware of your surroundings. They are a reflection of the life you are creating for yourself.

MAKING A SHIFT

Dr. Wayne Dyer talks about "the shift"; a change human beings make based on an epiphany or major life experience. I interpret it as, when we are ready to open up, opportunities for awareness and growth are available. Then we can make a shift, which will enrich and change our lives. I look for opportunities to learn and grow each day and the Externship experience is offering many challenges based on my fears and weaknesses, which allow me to look them in the face and say Thank You for the opportunity; another Dr. Dyer recommendation. Man, it's not easy to say the least, but the beauty in this experience has really been deepened by incorporating that concept. Linda Parelli says, "life is perfect" and I've been so inspired by her ability to remain in that space and mindset with things that must have been so challenging. She gives gratitude for every experience. I view Linda as a balanced, evolved human being who sets the standard for the type of human being and woman I aspire to become. So, I look for her approach to things in life and focus on those as areas I want to grow in and strategies I make an effort to incorporate. Over the years, I've had some challenges that felt overwhelming that brought great beauty and big gifts to my life. However, I wasn't able to see that going in, and ended up in the dark time after time. Often, Linda's writings and words would come to mind when I would be at the darkest part of the experience. "Life is Perfect" or "The dark comes before the dawn" concepts are things I have not only read or heard Linda say, but the witnessing of her living this philosophy impacted me enough that it helped me pull myself up by the bootstraps and begin to look for the gifts and accept that each experience was/is exactly what I needed. These many gifts have brought me to a place where I now look for the gifts in each challenge. Oprah Winfrey says lessons show up as whispers and we sometimes need a brick upside the head to finally get it. Well, I've had a few of those and am finally looking for the gift in challenges.

I came into the Externship course with a plan to look for gratitude in each personal challenge and I am happy to say I've been able to find that gratitude and have had many opportunities to be challenged. For me, a big challenge is public speaking, especially in front of my peers and mentors here at the Parelli Ranch. I have set my sights on growth in this area while I'm here and Teri Sprague 4 Star Parelli Professional, and Externship coach extraordinaire, provides an amazing environment of stretching but not pushing so I am constantly able to stay in the growing zone and not reach the edge of the cliff. Such mastery as a teacher is inspiring and a wonderful opportunity to learn by watching her approach each day. I have reflected on the cause of my nerves around presenting and believe that, at the root of it is a lack of belief in myself. This is something I've been challenging myself to overcome through this past year, as I turned 35 and realized that was the area I needed to really focus on to move forward with the life I desire and require for myself. So, back to "the shift". A shift appears to me to be a moment when openness, desire to grow, and reaching the ability to be grateful for the challenges and fears all come together and opportunities or connections show up with other humans (and, for me, horses present these opportunities often times). A shift is true awareness and absorption of the lesson to a place that resonates deep into our soul. Getting it on a level that even our brains can't get in the way of. However, our minds have to be open and seeking to allow it to happen. Two things happened recently that brought a shift for me. Mark Weiler read my blog and it resonated with him. He reached out to connect with me on that. He embraced me with genuine care that felt like we've been family forever and in such a way that I can only describe as being so authentic, self aware, and clear on his life's passion and goals in a human being that it shows up the moment you are in their presence. This was a moment of being changed for the better by being in the presence of an "eagle". This will make more sense if you read my last blog "soaring with eagles". The second experience, two days after connecting with Mark was sitting down for my mid term interview with Teri and Ann Kiser. Two more "eagles" that embody the beauty of Parelli as a lifestyle, a family, and a program and that exemplify the ability to become the best me I can be through the Parelli journey and remain authentically, uniquely who they are. They are in the group of people I look to for guidance and inspiration on how to become the human I want to be and become more authentically me, to live the most fulfilling life I can. The interview consisted of honest feedback on my progress and input on where I'm at. They answered my questions openly and honestly and I was so honored and grateful to have their time, energy, and genuine caring in sitting down with me. A shift has occurred for me regarding my challenge this year on believing in myself and loving myself. The experiences all three of these amazing human beings brought to me went much deeper than words. Knowing they mean what they say and respecting each of them as I do brought an opportunity for my soul to believe I do deserve to be here. I have known for a while that Parelli is a way of life for me and is the journey that will continue to help me become the human being I want to be. This program resonates with me in all the areas of life that matter for me; my values, passion for horses, desire for consistent self growth, and many other genuine interests and beliefs. To be at the Parelli Ranch, in the Externship, and have these three amazing people give me the feedback they did brought a shift in my heart, my soul, and even my brain that I am a part of this family. I am still processing, but I can tell you that moment by moment a change is happening for me deep inside that is showing up as true inner confidence and self love. I believe this is due to my clarity on Parelli being the lifestyle and pathway for me in all key areas that are important for me. Experiencing yet again, but in a bigger way, that Parelli is all about changing the world for horses and humans has brought a shift in my life experience that will enrich and change me forever. Gratitude doesn't begin to express how I feel. I have a sense of calm joy and knowledge that this is a big step that will show up as growth in many areas of my life. This is big, really big, but I'm not surprised. It's what Parelli does, is all about, and I am so excited to be a Parelli Professional, and go out into the world and pay it forward. Here's to you making a shift. Find the beauty in every challenge and the gift in each mistake.

ENDING = ONLY THE BEGINNING

As I prepare to leave Pagosa and move into the next part of my journey, I am reflecting on something our instructor 4 Star Parelli Professional Teri Sprague left us with. "Every Ending is the beginning of a new beginning. Welcome to the new beginning." For me, each experience in life is an opportunity to learn and grow and I am committed to living with the "life is perfect" belief system every day. Linda Parelli came to speak to us on graduation day and was inspiring and thought provoking as usual. I was moved by her words as well as her way of being. With the final emotional, beautiful sharing of highlights, gratitudes, and fun times as we had cake and ice cream in the barn, I have been moved to write to you to share more on this amazing journey.

...A new beginning. On first thought, that means to me expansion on my business as a Parelli Professional and my horsemanship. As I let it sink in a bit, there's way more to it. For each of us, it will be different depending on what we need to learn. Linda talked about how, over the years, she's seen people go through this experience and it can be difficult, emotionally. She gave us guidance on how we can take the opportunity to learn rather than spread discomfort or negative thoughts to those around us. We can stop and realize we are at a point in our journey that's hard and choose to manage ourselves and be in it, rather than place blame on others or decide it's all been bad. I've been processing for the last couple of weeks with the ending of the externship coming and it has felt like I've truly had two little voices having constant conversations on managing me.

..."I wonder what my outcome will be. Remain in the present. But I'm so curious about my next step."

You get the picture.

Also, I am a true Right Brained Extrovert and am so aware of my inclination to need approval from others. That has been something I've committed to managing while in the externship. I've been able to keep those moments to a minimum and not allow them to take me off course, but they are still there. As Linda talked yesterday, I thought more about the reality that we don't become someone else through learning and growth. We continue to become a better version of who we are, innately. This year, my 35th, I realized my biggest challenge and need was to be whole; from within. Authentically. I recognize moments when there's a difference in how I come to the table based on where I am on that scale. As a Right Brained Extrovert, I may find myself more focused on getting praise from the outside than I'd like. This time here at the externship has given me many opportunities to see the growth I've made there as well as many opportunities to feel the feelings and pull myself away from what I consider unhealthy reactions that can too easily take me to a place of judging, expecting others to fill me up, and so on. Interestingly, I have had outside praise from people who I respect and trust that has helped me find a deeper place inside of me that fills me up. With every big lesson, I discover life is not neat and tidy and usually things are not black and white. I am aware that I will be processing this experience for a long while, but am currently very clear that I have found significant growth from deep in my soul. My next big challenge for myself is to work at becoming a great presenter. A presenter that can engage others and be there for them, not concerned about myself. For this Right Brained Extrovert that will be quite a feat and I am ready for the challenge. This will mean such learning and growth in confidence and I will be able to better engage in making the world a better place for horses and humans as part of the Parelli mission. I commit to living with the "I am" feeling of being there (meaning being where I want to be) as Dr. Wayne Dyer talks about in his book "wishes fulfilled". I leave with a peacefulness I don't remember ever feeling. A knowingness that I am on the cusp of something big and that will come from within me. My genuine wish for you is that you find the areas of your life where you need the biggest growth and that will be the most challenging and dive in (or tiptoe in depending on what works for you). Those are the biggest opportunities to have the most amazing shifts and get closer to being the most authentic, successful, whole version of yourself.

The title of this next chapter came out of a conversation between my Mom, an old friend of hers, Nashville musician, businessman, and song writer, Randy Galloway, his wife Carol, and me. I went to Nashville to spend the weekend with my Mom on my way home from Pagosa Springs (around my elbow to get to my thumb...but necessary). We had some deep conversations on life, which I LOVE, and Randy described these times in life as "pivot points". Thanks for succinctly putting that in words, Randy!

PIVOT POINTS

There are times in our lives when we find ourselves with big decisions to make due to unforeseen circumstances or situations where we've done everything we could, but the outcome is different than we had hoped. These are pivot points. As Jim Patterson who offered a Play to Win workshop during the Externship course told us, we can STOP, CHALLENGE, AND CHOOSE our response. STOP to think about our thoughts, words, and reactions and really notice what the attitude we have is. CHALLENGE any negative attitude and patterns of behavior we might have begun to fall into. CHOOSE to move forward with the thoughts, actions, and attitude that will help us get a better result. I've had some big opportunities since returning home from the Externship a month ago to utilize the things Jim taught us. A chain of events that I know have big meaning has occurred, and I find myself selling a home, required to find a new home in 30 days, get creative with a business to find infusion of funds and keep my horsemanship on track to Level 4 so I can activate my 2 Star License so I can continue following my dreams. I've had experiences in the past, especially through 7 years of opening and owning a business, that have provided opportunities to learn to accept big challenges and scary times I couldn't control. I find myself reflecting on all that has been put before me now and looking more from a place of wondering what the lesson is and what the message is. I truly believe every experience in life is as it should be to teach us what we need to learn and similar experiences keep coming around if we continue to need the lesson. Also, as I go through life and watch the experiences of myself and others, it seems that big challenges sometimes arise so we can reflect on growth and recognize where we've come.

As I have this experience, I continually see that I can STOP worrying patterns, CHALLENGE any assumptions or distress and CHOOSE to find constant gratitude, believe my journey will unfold as it is supposed to, and be in the now versus constantly thinking about someday. This has become my focus rather than the specifics of the situation. I think of as, "it's not about the..." we learn from Linda Parelli. By doing this, I'm able to often find the thought "How interesting" floating through my mind. The truth is I go in and out of the place I want to be as well as the place fear can take me to in my mind, but I am aware this is the reality of our life's journey.

I have discovered that, through writing, I connect with so many of you and a big part of my journey is to continue to do that in a way that resonates or inspires and to be open and ready for your responses, which resonate and inspire me so much. To share the ups and downs and the reality of this journey and the school of life is my passion, which I know is the biggest reason Parelli is the core of my dream.

I am at a major pivot point in my life where some big areas are coming together to change in what feels like a bit of a whirlwind. I am committed to standing outside it as often as possible and looking in with wonder, allowing it to unfold, while remaining active and engaged. My daily goal is to look for the lessons and the directions the Universe is giving me. To let it all unfold without trying to control everything, but to allow the pieces of the puzzle to fall into place perfectly, which looks messy and chaotic at times. My attitude and outlook is my choice and I keep a strong focus on that. When things like money, a home, our family's happiness, and a place for animals we love are in question, the biggest opportunities to focus on the perfection of each moment, each experience, and each challenge are there.

As I go through this pivot point in my life, I think about writing to connect with others who have stories of pivot points and asking others to share pivot points in their life and how those brought them to the place they are. My hope is that by opening up and sharing, others will be strengthened if facing challenging times in their lives, as well. What are some pivot points you've faced in your life? How have they been a gift and how did you go through those experiences? Here's to life's biggest uncertainties; for they are the moments that give us strength, clarity, and the beautiful opportunities to be the best of who we are.

Life is THE Master Class

What a whirlwind the last few weeks have been; Or seemed to have been. I unexpectedly found myself in a position where I was looking for a new home and moving within 40 days. My initial outlook and commitment was to surrender and allow for all the lessons that would come, as well as move forward with gratitude and emotional fitness. My husband and I were clear on what each of our personal challenges might be and were ready to honor and learn from those. Things I've learned through the Parelli Program, once again, were central aspects of how I would not only get through this but "enjoy the ride" and learn tons. Of course there were also many moments of inner struggle when I was not, at that moment, able to remain in balance, emotionally. I forgive myself for that and recognize it as part of my journey to growth.

I generally look for a key lesson with life's experiences. There have been so many, but here's a BIG one.

When we feel challenged by something, emotionally, that is the very thing that tells us what we need to look for in ourselves as the area we need to face and find growth.

The beautiful thing about this is that we can get MAJOR GROWTH from the BIGGEST CHALLENGES.

Now, finding the balance between facing our fears and challenges and pushing ourselves over the cliff is another art in itself.

We are now settling into our new home where I feel at peace and connected; inspired to write and continue growth within myself and with my horse. I'll be able to grow our food, have our hens all around and sit in the afternoon sun at the beach or in the yard just being...

The community here is a supportive, connected one, where neighbors put out avocados on the corner with a sign that says "avos 70 cents" and a bucket where you put your money; the honor system.

In some ways, I feel like I've gone back to my little home town in Western North Carolina; certainly back to my roots. I know I've come home. What's the definition of home? Like most horse questions the answer to this life question is "it depends". For me, home is being connected to my life's purpose, loving and honoring that, believing in it and committing myself to it so that I may feel at peace and keep my passion.

The things I mentioned about this new home we were guided to are all connected to my soul path and my life purpose. Life is perfect.

What are the major challenges you have faced or are facing? What are the big opportunities and lessons available to you?

...with gratitude that I may share my passion with you...may you find your home wherever you are

Aloha

Smiling Counts

"Smiling Counts". I can't count the number of times I heard our Externship Instructor, 4 Star Parelli Professional, Teri Sprague say that this summer. I find myself recounting those words constantly in my day to day life and it has become a mantra that helps me in so many situations.

When with my horse and I find a moment where I'm unsure or start to feel at a loss, I hear Teri's words and put a big smile on my face.

When I'm with my horse playing with a pattern or focusing on progression and I realize I may be getting a bit serious, I hear Teri's words and put a big smile on my face.

This has trickled out into the rest of my life to so many other moments.

If I'm driving and find myself in traffic or am in line somewhere and begin to worry about whether I'll get to my next destination, I hear Teri's words and smile.

If I'm with my husband and we begin to take a conversation in the direction of friction, I hear Teri's words and put a big smile on my face. It makes a change in me and will often make him smile too.

Sometimes when I'm doing my daily chores at the ranch I'll realize I'm not feeling too positive about it. I hear Teri's words and smile. I can then look around and see the beauty all around me and find gratitude.

Hearing Teri's words and physically smiling as genuinely as I can muster. That simple thing changes my state. I've heard Tony Robbins talk about how we need to sometimes change our state by doing something physical and this is something that works for me.

I've been reflecting on how big an impact a person or experience can have on our lives and this is one of many lessons from the Externship that make me realize how valuable that experience was. To say it was life changing is an understatement. These are life lessons that I absorbed so deeply that it comes to me when I need it in a way that has changed the stories I was telling myself, and change my thoughts at the deepest level; which has a domino effect of changing my words, actions, and character.

I have such a since of gratitude and pleasure when I'm with a horse and recognize that I am truly changed for the better. My confidence, abilities and skills have all grown in ways that I know come from being immersed in a place that is focused on growth, emotional fitness, and learning. Removing the worries of day to day life and being surrounded by others who share a passion in this type of environment offers such opportunities. I find myself in awe sometimes as I further recognize the huge value of this experience that continues to show up in my daily life in new ways.

I have clarity that it will continue to show up in various ways and look forward to experiences every year at the Parelli Center as I continue my education and growth.

My hope is to share this nugget of gold from Teri and that you'll find her words as valuable as I have.

May you find moments when you can hear those words and it can make a change for you.

..."smiling counts".

Hunker Down

"HUNKER DOWN" This is a phrase I grew up using in the US Southeast.

We played a game during the Fast Track Course at the Parelli Center in Florida, called Hunker Down, where we stood on buckets and used the 45' rope to try and pull each other off our bucket. Thinking back to my childhood and the phrase "hunker down" I got really low; almost on my heels and settled in on that bucket.

"Hunker Down" has become a mantra for me lately and taken on even bigger meaning. When we look around at mother nature, there are so many wonderful examples of hunkering down being an instinctual thing.

The ocean ebs and flows. The tides come and go. A huge swell may come in with big thunder crashing waves or a gnarly current may come where people, all too often, are taken out and lose their lives. Then it's all over and the ocean is back to that quiet, serene, picture of relaxation many of us see as a great way to help us sleep or meditate.

Recently, two wild roosters in our yard fought and one seemed on death's door. He disappeared for a week or so while life went on all around us. Then, today, he showed up again. No muss, no fuss. Just a part of the flock.

Three cats were born on our property that I took on the responsibility of care for. Two of them always come to eat and stick pretty close. One of them is more skittish and seems to like to explore. He shows up when he shows up. I can either worry and stress about whether he's okay, or "hunker down" and just let it be. I can purposefully choose my thoughts and create a constant state of excitement or worry or I can just do what mother nature does and allow.

My horse had a on again off again lameness issue for a long time that I couldn't figure out. I tried bodywork, nutrition research and changes, essential oils, red light, an animal communicator, shimming the saddle, shoeing, trimming, etc etc etc. Then, I went away for 3 months to the Parelli Center for an Externship and came back to a completely healthy comfortable horse, with no body issues. Hmmm. Next time I'm dealing with something like this, I may incorporate simply leaving my horse alone and letting her get a little fat with no responsibilities (and not being constantly surrounded by my worrying energy) as a part of her healing program.

The way I see hunker down now, is to sit back and allow. Allow things to happen as they will and remain in a mindful state of emotional fitness. Things happen; life goes on. Hunker down and observe rather than try to control. Be mindful of your state of mind. As I experiment with this, I see the difference in what type of experiences shape up around me, depending on my state of mind. It's part of that quote we hear from Pat Parelli, "Be careful of your thoughts, they create your words. Be careful of your words, they create your actions. Be careful of your actions, they create your character. You and I are two of life's characters, so be careful of your thoughts." That may not be the quote word for word, but the meaning is so resonant.

Purpose borne leadership

The past couple of weeks I've been contemplating my plans and personal growth needs along with skills needed for me to be able to complete my Level 4 auditions with my horse. One theme that has been prevalent is my leadership. There have been moments when my horse (a true Left Brained Introvert) has spooked big and taken off. I wondered, "how did that happen?" There have been moments when my horse wouldn't connect to me and try. There have also been moments when my horse offered HUGE things before I even asked. At this stage of our journey, we've experienced a lot of things together and thanks to Horsenality and Humanality I have some blue prints and fact based formulas I can use to help assess what's happening with her and with me.

While contemplating the differences in each session, my horse and I had a job to do. The cattle needed to be moved and we were given the opportunity to do it by ourselves; a really exciting first! The herd was ready to move and the moment we entered the pasture they were coming toward us, calling and ready. I didn't have time to think or worry or plan. I had to rely on all that I've learned from the gentleman who has given me this incredible opportunity, whom I've been so blessed to spend time with the last few years.

My horse thought she'd like to eat some Keawe beans, but I knew if we didn't keep a nice flow, the cattle could disperse in the alley or start going through fences so I simply had to require her to stay with me and move forward.

The clamp clamp clamp of all the hooves behind us sounding like a storm coming and the herd calling back as I gave the calls they know to follow rattled her a bit, but I had to keep her with me. I said to her, "we've got a job to do and you can trust me; now move forward". I was mindful to use the lightest phase possible, but do what was necessary. I remembered to smile to keep my disposition where I wanted it. I was mindful of being consistent so my horse knew I'd continue to be fair. I heard the voice of my teacher when she'd go to stop to try to get grass or spook a bit, reminding me there's more at stake here; and I'd get re committed to doing this job the way he's taught me and get the cattle to the new pasture as a complete herd, calmly, with none going through fences or being left behind.

I'd have little moments where I might start to wonder, "what if I screw this up"? But I'd snap myself out of it, knowing I didn't have time to go there and reminding myself that I know what to do; he's taught me.

At one point, wild pigs came running from the grasses and she got high headed, then a nearby gate was swinging in the wind and she really got tense like she might consider running. However, we had a job to do and the cattle were beginning to stop and I knew that meant they might start turning around or going through fences if I didn't keep ahead of them, calling. So, I picked up a steady rein and lightly used the "bother bother" method with my spur as I put my hand on her whither. I think I said out loud to her, "I got this, you can trust me; but we have a job to do so please come back to me". And she did.

The gentleman whom I've been lucky enough to learn about cattle from these past few years came and we did a sweep of the original pasture looking for calves or any of the herd that may not have made the move; there were none. We went back to close all the gates and ride through the herd then sat later talking about horses and horsemanship and I thanked him for giving me the responsibilities that day.

I had realized how important putting Principles to Purpose really is. I've been so thankful to have a purpose for my horse, but on this day I realized just how important having a purpose, a goal that matters to me, is for me as a leader.

I take pride in getting the job done with cattle in a calm, mindful way. I am passionate about them and about my horse being my partner in that. It matters to me that a man who has given his time and energy to teach me sees I have been a good student and have learned what he has offered. At the very depths of my soul I want to always be able to think that if my horse's mother was there she'd be smiling as she watched me with her baby, as I've heard Pat Parelli talk about.

Putting myself in a situation where I have goals that really are important to me helps me dig up the leadership I need to get it done.

I went back through the Parelli Mastery Lesson DVDs and watched a lesson where Linda Parelli coached a protege' on clarity in transitions between gaits and during the session her horse began to spook. Linda coached her to keep at it and the horse re connected with her. I had read a blog where another protege' recounted a similar lesson from

Linda before and I needed to get that second hand gold again. I was able to absorb it more this time.

Next time I'm in the arena playing with patterns or out in the field riding with obstacles and my horse begins to spook or take over, I'm gonna remember that recent day where I recognized what the leader in me had to look like to convince her I was worth being followed.

The part I'm most proud of about that ride, is that I never got frustrated with my horse. I was able to remain in a constant state of emotional awareness and think about what my horse needed from me while getting the job done. As a predominant Right Brained Extrovert, this is a big accomplishment.

As I further contemplate this beautiful lesson, I think about the areas of my life where I've had to dig deep and find strength in leadership to get something accomplished that mattered to me or simply had to get done. The lessons really are everywhere and Parelli really is way more than riding. I am in awe, yet again, recognizing that because of Parelli I am on the path to becoming the human being I want to be. With horse and in life

Life is perfect revisited & Self Love

This nugget of wisdom we hear from Linda Parelli is one of those that is helpful in just about any situation or challenge life presents, I'm finding. I think of how growth in life is all about pulling back the layers and I'm at a place where I'm absorbing the "life is perfect" lesson in so many new ways and, I hope, at a much deeper level. Also, I marvel at how other life lessons and mantras flow into this one and when I can tap into them I see real progress and success. My measure of success is seeing growth within myself in every life experience; seeing even 1% more progress toward becoming the human being I want to be.

When I turned 35 almost a year ago I had a realization that I could continue working on growth in so many areas, as I had been doing for well over a decade, or I could focus on the thing I saw I had been avoiding because it was the most painful and so scary; I lacked real love for myself. I began looking around at people and seeing that the people who had what I wanted had a self assuredness that makes the real difference. What I realized was that when self love is authentic, a person operates from such a different place than when self love isn't present. The difficult, scary thing I had to be honest about was that I didn't have that and it affected every thought, word, and action I made and created my character. I was walking through life studying all these self help books and creating mantras and vision boards to create the life I wanted. But at my core I was lacking the very thing that would make or break whether I began living the life I really wanted. If I didn't get that sorted out, the lack of self love would keep me finding myself in a cycle that, though it involved lots of achievements, growth and experiences, also continued to be steeped in so much fear, worry, and coming short of where I wanted to be. I looked outside myself for acceptance. It took me years to be able to see this and it was so hard because it hit home so deeply. How interesting that life brought me to a place where I found my passion through Parelli and that very thing that I am most committed to and love the most is the place where I found myself unable to take chances or operate in ways that would undoubtedly bring me much further along in my journey. Over the past 3 years, I've been to the Parelli Centers multiple times and after last summer at the Externship, I got really clear on this lack of authentic love of self and how it was holding me back. Though there were so many things to celebrate and beautiful relationships created, I knew I was holding back in some areas due to fear.

All my life I've been able to be ballsy and take chances; I'm an entrepreneur (and an Aries, as well as a Right Brained Extrovert), I jump into things with both feet without abandon. I couldn't wrap my mind around this one. I struggled with why I found myself consistently stopping short of doing or saying things out of fear, while at the Centers. I had finally found my true passion that I knew would be a part of my journey for the rest of my life and I couldn't find that woman who I'd always been; or told myself I was. I had a belief that when you find your passion, you are great at it and it will "flow". Well, I now know that finding the things we love truly can bring out our biggest personal challenges and fears. The potential turning point presents our options which are, face the fear and move through it or avoid the fear and fall back to living the same life we always have. Sometimes I have to just sit and look at the fear and be brave enough not to turn and run, but would be pushing myself over an emotional cliff if I stepped through the fear at that moment. I am grateful to have begun the part of my journey where I will find the biggest desires and see my biggest inner challenges, as I know this will help me grow by leaps and bounds. It will require, however, for me to remember that facing my fears is absolutely necessary to continue my journey in creating the life I crave; the life my soul craves. I have a deep commitment to live with no regrets every day. My soul craves a life where I help others find authentic self and growth. I must make myself vulnerable and be willing to look at my biggest fears and personal challenges to be able to fill and fulfill my soul. For me, sharing those vulnerabilities and discoveries with all of you is an integral part of my journey. I'm discovering that being honest with myself, then sharing with others who connect on this journey and desire to consistently grow is a beautiful way to help me face my challenges and fears; this biggest one being realization that every thought and action I take is directly related to my growth of finding self love and acceptance.

For the last year, I have been seeking and committed to tools to help me continually look at whether my actions come from self acceptance or needing acceptance from the outside. In many instances faking it til I make it works, but when those moments of recognition of self love show up, it's akin to how it feels for me when I'm with a horse and feel a soul connection that comes only with putting the relationship first, as the Parelli program teaches us. I am finding the biggest changes of my life from the inside and have been moved to share this with you. It feeds my soul to do so and I truly hope something in my sharing resonates with you on some level. I am so grateful for this supportive community who share guidelines, principles, and core values. We are each forever changed for having this incredible community and a place to connect with so many others whose souls resonate. I find myself, yet again, in awe of this beautiful program, business, and family Pat and Linda Parelli have created and how the world is changing every moment of every day because of the people making inner changes due to the Parelli program. Beautiful. THANK YOU

You gotta know when to hold 'em...

Do you know the song "the gambler" by Kenny Rogers? I grew up listening to that song and recently revisited it. I was searching itunes for something for a play session with my horse and saw "the gambler". I decided to download it and set off to play. Well, that song and the play sessions to follow inspired this blog. I am preparing for Level 4 auditions with Taxi, the Left Brained Extrovert gelding in my life, and started with Online play. The song had great meaning during the session because I was highly aware of the moments when I needed to stop and wait for him when he was learning something new. This doesn't match his normally very Left Brained Extrovert horsenality, but it's very important for him that I wait in those moments. While I was waiting the song was playing on my iPhone..."if you're gonna play the game boy, you gotta learn to play it right. You gotta know when to hold 'em, know when to fold 'em, know when to walk away and know when to run". It was resonating with me and I began thinking about how much it applies to horsemanship. I looked at Taxi and thought about knowing when to hold 'em and knowing when to fold 'em and all that could sum up. I thought about feeling during the day and thinking at night, as Pat Parelli talks about and set off to honor what the song was talking about; bringing everything I've learned to the table and trusting that I have it within me to offer Taxi what he needs. After playing for a bit, we headed to the big arena for Liberty Play; our first session in an open area. I took off the halter and planned to let him relax while I set up cones. He came with me. I smiled and offered a little stick to me, he was super connected and offered to circle me at trot, then canter. "All right, game on", I thought. "Let's play". We cantered around the arena, I asked for circling he offered it, I asked for fig 8 around the cones, he said yes. We played stick to me all around the rail of the arena with circles peppered in. Then I'd run away and he'd gallop toward me stopping when I turned and put up my hand. We played with the yo yo pattern, then canter to me and lead by the tail. We were on fire and I was laughing with pure enjoyment. The song kept playing. "Every gambler knows, that the secret to surviving...is knowing what to throw away and knowing what to keep. Cause every hand's a winner and every hand's a loser..." Hmmm. Every horseman knows, that the secret to partnership is knowing what to throw away and knowing what to keep. This song got me inspired to not only think about, but feel the concepts of taking what the horse is offering, letting the horse set the timeline, knowing when to wait and when to do something...and knowing what that something is based on what the horse is telling us. I could really feel the meaning of Pat Parelli's words, "know where to be, when to be and why to be and what to do when you get there...and when to stop doing what you're doing". I took this fun correlation and the song with me to my Left Brained Introvert mare and it was maybe even more resonant there. She needs very different things than Taxi does, and I have to soften my energy and do a lot of setting it up and waiting, waiting, waiting, and agreeing. The song helped me turn sessions into a "can you" set up for me. Can you honor the 4 responsibilities of the human that Parelli teaches? For me, there is a resonant message in knowing what to throw away and knowing what to keep...every hand's a winner and every hand's a loser...depending on the human. Music has such an impact on mood and energy for me that I am inspired to share with you a bit of my process when a song really takes hold. And it helps me honor the Parelli Value "Get it done with a little fun".

Hurry Up and Wait - 100 cattle became my teachers

Hurry Up and Wait is something we used to say when I was in the US Air Force. At that time the phrase had a specific meaning for me. It wasn't a positive thing. It was a way to complain. The feeling was that we were expected to hurry, hurry, hurry, but then no, wait! Suffice it to say my attitude and outlook on life was different than it is today. I was looking for reasons to complain versus reasons to celebrate. That was before Parelli entered my life.

Hurry Up and Wait has come to me recently, again, but with a completely different resonance. I'd like to share a story.

I was preparing to move the cattle to a new pasture by setting up gates in my vehicle, with the plan to tack up and bring my horse back to get them moved. At this point my horses and I had been working alone with the cattle for about 6 weeks and the herd was getting comfortable with us on a different level. Prior to this experience, the cattle were comfortable with me when I was on my horse, but definitely not comfortable with me if I came along on foot. They would scatter. Well, that has changed. Here's how it unfolded.

As I was setting up gates the cows were calling and moving to the gate that would give them access to the new pasture they'd be rotating to. An idea began to take shape in my mind. I decided to open the gate and begin to allow them to enter, then come back on my horse. I made the assumption that when I drove down to the gate and stepped out of my vehicle on foot they'd scatter or at least move away, as they've done in the past. Well, that didn't happen. The events that followed required me to operate from feel and instinct with no time to analyze or really think. I stepped out of my vehicle and went to open the gate. The cattle stayed put, calling and ready to move through the gate. Hmmm. I went with it. I opened the gate and stepped out of the way, behind the gate so as to remove my "blow horns" as Linda Parelli describes, and keep my energy from blocking or driving them. I was sure to have a soft energy and a smile. Through the gate they came. This blew my mind. It began to look like this would be an easy move. Ha! There was a lesson about to come for me.

A group of calves got blocked; they are usually more sensitive and were not able to be confident coming through with me standing there. So at this point, a few calves were apart from the main herd and I now really wanted to accomplish the move on foot. It had become a possibility and I wanted to figure this out. I quickly moved through the gate back to my vehicle and went behind my vehicle facing away from the calves and leaving the gate opening for them in hopes they'd be drawn to their Mamas strongly enough to go through.

Here's where it began to get interesting. The calves were still a bit stuck. I saw the main herd start to come back toward me and the gate like a big wave. Have you ever seen a herd when they begin moving as one? It's really beautiful and powerful. Like the ocean.

Remember, I was now committed to the idea that I could move the herd on foot on this day and when I saw the herd coming back toward the gate, I recognized that might not happen. So I started acting quickly, but with a focus on remaining thoughtful and emotionally fit. There were definitely safety concerns. with me on foot and over 100 livestock coming toward me with zeal. I stepped into the gate opening and brought my energy up, lifting my hand; all blow horns as strong as I could muster. They stopped. Wow. "But go on, Cryshtal, no time to waste, they are ready to move". The calves were still behind me, separated from their Mamas. If I couldn't get them through all together, they'd go back into the old pasture and I'd have to wait until another time for them to be ready and willing to move again. I started walking to the new pasture, toward the next gate opening, they turned and followed me.

At this point, I consciously realized I was on foot in a large open space with a herd of more than 100 livestock following me. I looked around to check fences I might run to and climb should I find myself in trouble. I then looked behind me and one of the Black Bulls was trotting toward me; okay. The thoughts and emotions that came up for me in that moment are indescribable. The bull had the expression of a puppy dog, ready to follow. Logically, I got that he wasn't coming AT ME or AFTER ME, but OMG! This huge bull was trotting toward me and I was on foot. The next thought that came to me was GO! Well, I also saw some humor in it, seeing him with his ears flopping, trotting to me. I thought to myself, "only you would get yourself into this situation, Cryshtal". I began to run, laughing, to the next gate opening and prepared to get on or behind the gate and let them go through. I stepped to the side, the herd stopped and looked at me. It was the same look our horses get when they begin asking questions. So I took a deep breath, realizing they were with me, but not overexcited, and walked with purpose on through and toward the next gate.

To ensure they'd stay in the new pasture I was looking for them to begin to scatter and start eating. They were still concentrated on me, so I kept walking forward. They kept following.

Some eventually began moving out of the herd and began eating.

I kept walking since many were still following and headed toward the last gate we'd go through where grass was really tall, knowing they'd be happy to start eating when they got to this area.

Here's the Wait part of this Hurry Up and Wait experience. A handful of cows who are very sensitive ended up separated as the more confident cows had gone through this last gate. I was standing next to the gate opening, waiting for them to go through. I recognized they wanted to go through, but couldn't. They stood there, doing approach and retreat, but couldn't make it. I softened my energy, experimenting with what it would take to help them be comfortable. And I waited.

Did I mention I'm Right Brained Extrovert cusp Left Brained Extrovert? Waiting is such a beautiful challenge for me; it doesn't come natural.

I looked at my watch so I could time how long it actually took, knowing it would feel like an eternity keeping my feet (and mind) still.

I recognized the cows wouldn't be able to come through with me being that close to the opening, no matter how soft my energy was so I gently turned and walked further away, remaining soft and keeping a gentle smile on my face...breathing out consciously; moving slow without being sneaky.

I moved away until I noticed them get a bit "unstuck" then stopped and waited. I didn't need to do anything but ALLOW them to find comfort and confidence to go through the gate to their herd, where they wanted to be. Eventually they went through and the entire herd began happily grazing. I could go back to my car and close the gate to the old pasture.

I took a moment to take in the beautiful surroundings.

I was on foot, alone, standing on the ground, connected to the earth and all the surroundings of mother nature; the tall grasses, the cattle, the birds singing, the breeze. Nothing to do but give gratitude in that moment.

I took the long walk back to my vehicle, in awe at the experience I'd just had, contemplating the life lessons and realizing the entertainment someone might have gotten if they had been watching.

If you are a student of Parelli Natural Horsemanship, you'll have recognized the many areas of this story where I've been given amazing tools, knowledge, and strategies from the Parelli Program and utilized them to find a successful outcome.

The one thing I've been reflecting on most, however, is a new way to look at Hurry Up and Wait. I realized the concept is actually a wonderful, simple, thought. There are moments in life when I'll need to Hurry Up and there are moments when I'll need to Wait. The key is having the confidence in myself, the feel, and the emotional fitness to recognize what each moment calls for and be able to honor that need. This 20 minute experience on that day showed me I can trust myself and taught me a bit more about the concept that was presented to me so many years ago, in the Air Force. Seems like a lifetime has passed and it doesn't feel like it could've been me; that person who was looking for ways to complain. But it was. I've grown, I've changed. Through my commitment to the Parelli Program; the Parelli Tribe, I've found a new way to look at life and see the lessons all around me. This is the juicy part. There is no getting THERE, I am already HERE. To quote Linda Parelli again, "Life is Perfect". Here's to your journey.

Simply Allow...

My time with the horses has been focused on our job with the cattle lately, and oh what life lessons I've been offered! The cattle offer so many lessons, and they have been the biggest inspiration for this post.

The gentleman I've been honored to spend time learning from has taught me about using the psychology of the cows and setting up a situation for success. He talks about how important it is not to chase them, scare them, or cause them to want to run from you. Working with this herd reminds me of how important it is to allow life to unfold rather than think about how to control each moment. I've been getting many opportunities to WAIT and WATCH and OBSERVE. I'm reminded of how important it is to approach any conversation, whether it be with human or animal...any life experience...with the intention to engage and be present in the moment. That means understanding that I don't have the ability to know what the person is going to say or the ability to know what the horse or cows are gonna do. I must commit to being one piece of the conversation. This is a great lesson on the importance of Parelli principle #3. Communication is two or more individuals sharing an idea or understanding.

I can't preplan what I'll say or do if I really want to be effective and connected.

And I REALLY DO want to be connected and effective. I must be able to trust that I have within me the ability to offer something without the need to plan before hand. I have a solid foundation. I have a lot to offer. And, of course, there's the possibility that I won't have anything to offer at that moment or may not know what to offer depending on the question I'm asked or the situation I'm presented with by the cattle or the horses...or life. And that's okay. Life is perfect, as Linda Parelli says, and each moment is an opportunity to learn and grow.

I have the most success and progressive experiences with the horses, the cattle, and with people when

I'm able to focus on them, asking questions and really hearing their response.

With the cattle, there is a lot of setting it up and waiting. Sometimes I have no other option than to wait and see. What a super powerful opportunity to get comfortable being patient. If I set it up and have patience, I save myself lots of time and energy in the long run. As Pat Parelli teaches, I see the importance to "Take the time it takes so it will take less time". When it's time to move them, I need to prepare my timing so they are ready to go; best when they've come in for water or are all gathered in one area. If that's not the case I need to find them and begin calling until they show a desire to come with me. If there are calves that got separated and need to go through the gate, the best solution is for me to back off, give space, and WAIT for the calf to go to his mama. In other words, simply get out if the way; do nothing. Hmmm. Also, I've been given many opportunities to recognize how often I want to know if what I'm doing will work, right now. Wow. As much as I've worked on gaining patience, I've been given the beautiful gift of yet another mirror into myself. I am not where I want to be regarding having patience, trusting the process, being present in the moment and being able to really ALLOW the being I'm communicating with to be engaged. Daily, I am given opportunities to recognize this and progress. It's so interesting how powerful the mind is and how powerful our thought and behavior patterns are. Even when we have clarity and recognize an area we aspire to gain growth in, we can still fall back a bit into old patterns. I've come to look at these challenges for myself as the juicy part of life.

About The Author

Cryshtal Avera calls herself a soul seeker. She is passionate about looking for the lessons and gifts in each opportunity. Life has offered many opportunities for big lessons in Cryshtal's life from her childhood in Western North Carolina to her time in the US Air Force, as well as her experiences as a Real Estate Agent and Investor, a Small Business Owner and a horsemanship instructor. Her journey has become focused on following her bliss and looking to fulfill her soul's intended pathway as well as empowering others to do the same. She now offers what she calls Empowerment Coaching in the form of workshops along with private sessions, to help her clients heal and grow; looking for the opportunity to empower the individual to trust him/herself as well as using the powerful ability of the horse to help heal and reveal the truth in a way not most humans can't see alone or by being told. Cryshtal keeps a focus on being authentic and vulnerable as she writes to connect with others and offers gratitude for the opportunity to share her passion.

Contact Cryshtal or Learn More about her...

https://www.facebook.com/savvysoulseeker

www.parelliprohawaii.com

https://twitter.com/ParelliProHI

http://www.linkedin.com/pub/cryshtal-avera/36/728/382

Manufactured by Amazon.ca
Bolton, ON